HOW THIS BOOK CAN **HELP** YOU GET OUT OF A **STICKY SITUATION**

read on!

Read this bit first...!

Stranded on a desert island with only a box of cornflakes? Facing a grizzly bear, wondering how to persuade it that you will taste really yucky? Stuck in a hippo's jaws, wondering how you're going to going to get that homework done before tomorrow? We've all been there.

The problem is, when it comes to survival skills, everyone's an expert. Take the grizzly bear, for instance. Some people tell you that you should stare at a bear. Others say that it's better to RUN LIKE THE WIND. There are even a few who reckon that it's probably a good idea not to go anywhere near bears in the first place because then you won't need any survival skills to escape from them.

4

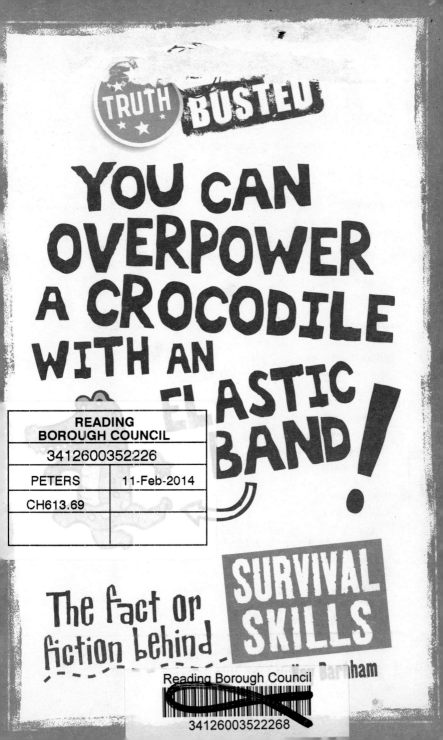

TRUTH BUSTED

YOU CAN
OVERPOWER
A CROCODILE
WITH AN
ELASTIC
BAND!

The fact or fiction behind **SURVIVAL SKILLS**

WAYLAND

Published in paperback in 2014 by Wayland

Wayland
338 Euston Road
London NW1 3BH

Wayland Australia
Level 17/207 Kent Street
Sydney, NSW 2000

Editor: Debbie Foy
Design: Rocket Design (East Anglia) Ltd
Illustration: Alan Irvine

Barnham, Kay.
The fact or fiction behind survival skills. -- (Truth or busted)
1. Survival--Juvenile literature. 2. Common fallacies--
Juvenile literature.
I. Title II. Series
613.6'9-dc23
ISBN: 987 0 7502 8157 7

Printed in Great Britain, by CPI Group (UK) Ltd, Croydon, CR0 4YY
10 9 8 7 6 5 4 3 2 1

Wayland is a division of Hachette Children's Books,
an Hachette UK company
www.hachette.co.uk

All illustrations by Shutterstock, except 4, 16, 35, 44, 53, 56, 76, 84-85, 90

So which tips do you believe and which do you totally ignore? Do you poke a shark in the eye or whack it on the nose? Will drinking your own wee stop you dying of thirst or poison you instead?

The first rule of survival is:

DON'T PANIC.

The second rule of survival is:

READ THIS BOOK.

Whether you want to find out about desert-island survival, grizzly bears, crocodiles, sharks or wee, you'll find it here. Top tips for what to do when an earthquake strikes or an avalanche hits? Yep. The best way to build an emergency shelter? That, too. Totally true survivors' tales? Sorted. Or maybe you just want to find which way is north so you can make it home in time for tea? Easy. (See page 34.)

So, don't panic. Just turn over the page...

read on!

> ## Cows are more deadly than great white sharks

This is clearly madness. Cows are gentle creatures that moo and sleep standing up and produce a gazillion litres of milk. Besides, they eat for EIGHT HOURS A DAY, so when would they have *time* to be deadly? Great white sharks are the bad guys here. Not cows.

★ And the truth is...

Yes. Yes, they are.

Sharks have a very bad press. Films and news stories about sharks ripping innocent swimmers to pieces have given these poor, misunderstood creatures a terrible reputation. Shark attacks do happen, but they are VERY rare. In 2011, for example, of the 118 shark attacks that were reported worldwide, only 17 people died.

Cows are a different matter. They are usually very docile, but if they feel threatened or if they think their calf is in danger, they will become aggressive. Between 2001 and 2009, 481 people were injured by cows and 18 people died *in the UK alone*.

Verdict: _____ TRUTH

To survive a shark attack, poke it in the eye

If you are one of the hundred-odd people who are unlucky enough to be attacked by a shark every year, what should you do to escape? Is it a good idea to poke a great white in the eye or is that going to make it REALLY mad?

★ And the truth is...

Go for it. If you poke a shark in the eye, it stuns the creature, which will let go of you and swim away. Or that's what they say. The problem is that, if you're thrashing about in the water, it's going to be quite difficult to find a shark's eye to poke. And if you wave an arm anywhere near an attacking shark's jaws, it's likely to bite it anyway. Experts reckon that a much better idea is to tap the shark on the nose (if you can find its nose, obviously). Sharks don't like this at all and will often just swim away. Oh, and keep calm. Because that's probably really easy to do when you're facing the scariest creature in the ocean...

Verdict: _____ **TRUTH** _____

DON'T DO THAT..

DON'T
swim with a box jellyfish.

Its sting is very, very poisonous and very, very deadly to humans. Oh, and don't expect it to look like a box. Or a wobbly jelly. Or, actually, a fish. It's just poisonous, right?

The box jellyfish is also known as a sea wasp or, to give it its proper scientific name, *Chironex fleckeri*. It is shaped like an umbrella, can swim as fast as 10 centimetres a second and has 24 eyes. Its tentacles, which can measure up to 3 metres long, are covered with very tiny harpoons that inject venom into its victims. Make sure you're not one of them.

DO THIS!

DO
swim with
bioluminescent
comb jellies.

Bioluminescent comb jellies are jelly-like sea creatures that look as if they might be related to jellyfish ... but aren't. Unbelievably, even though they look capable of delivering a sting that would stun a shark, comb jellies are not poisonous AT ALL. But they are a very beautiful bluey-green, with pink sparkles and multi-coloured stripes that glow in the dark so brightly you could probably consult your copy of *Truth or Busted: Survival Skills* by their light.

You can be surrounded by water and STILL die of thirst

No, no, no, no, no. How could that possibly happen? If you were cast adrift on a wooden raft in the middle of the Atlantic Ocean, totally surrounded by water, why would you NOT drink it?

Fancy a cuppa?

★ And the truth is...

Salty seawater is totally deadly and you should never drink it, not even when you're really, really thirsty. What happens is that your kidneys try to get rid of the salt in seawater by using the fresh water in your body to flush it away. And if you don't have enough water in your body, you become dehydrated, which can kill you. But rainwater is not salty at all. So if you're lost at sea, try to catch rainwater, either in a container or even in the folds of a waterproof coat. Drink that instead and you'll be fine. As long as you get spotted by a passing cruise liner, that is.

Verdict: TRUTH

I'm a survivor!

In 1942, Poon Lim was working on the SS *Ben Lomond* when it was torpedoed by a German submarine in the South Atlantic. The Chinese sailor jumped from the sinking ship, clambered aboard a life raft and then waited and waited and waited to be rescued. He waited a very long time. At first, Poon Lim ate and drank the supplies on board the life raft. But when the water, the biscuits, the chocolate and the sugar ran out, he used his homemade fishing rod – baited with a fish he'd hooked earlier – to catch a shark. And then he ate it. And, because it hadn't rained in a while, he drank the blood from its liver, too. At last, after a record-breaking 133 days at sea, he was rescued by Brazilian fishermen.

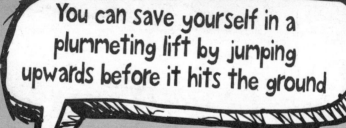

You can save yourself in a plummeting lift by jumping upwards before it hits the ground

It seems obvious, doesn't it? If a lift's mechanism breaks, all you need to do is jump into the air at the very last minute and then land, totally unharmed, after the impact.

⭐ And the truth is...

Er… no. Science is quite clear on this point. Jumping into the air won't help at all. If a lift were plummeting downwards, then you would be plummeting at exactly the same speed as the lift. If you *did* jump into the air, you might be plummeting at a *very* slightly slower speed, but you'd still be falling *very* quickly when the lift, and then you, hit the ground. Boom! But there's another problem. Lift floors aren't usually transparent, which means that you wouldn't be able to see the ground approaching and unless you knew the height of the lift shaft and were a top scientist who could work out how long it would take the lift to fall to the bottom, then how would you know when to jump in the first place? Tricky, huh?

'Get ready, JUMP!'

Verdict:

BUSTED

You can overpower a crocodile with an elastic band

But surely that's impossible? A crocodile has one of the most forceful bites on the planet. In fact, tests have revealed that a crocodile's chomp would rival the bite of the mightiest dinosaur of them all — the *Tyrannosaurus rex*. So how would an elastic band help?

⭐ And the truth is...

The muscles that a crocodile uses to open its jaws are much weaker than those that SNAP the jaws shut. It has to be a fairly sturdy elastic band, mind. But if you could get your elastic band around a crocodile's jaws, the chances are that it would then be quite difficult for the animal to open its mouth and chomp you. It's probably not a good idea to test the theory though.

Verdict:  TRUTH

HOW TO SURVIVE

...A HURRICANE

BEFORE A HURRICANE...

☆ Keep a close eye on the weather forecast.

☆ In case there's a power cut, make sure that you have a battery-operated radio, a torch and glow sticks. (For light, of course. It's no time to have a disco.)

☆ Board or tape up all windows.

☆ Tidy away or tie down anything that might take off in strong winds.

☆ If you're told to evacuate the area ... DO IT!

DURING A HURRICANE...

☆ Do not light candles.

☆ Stay away from windows.

☆ Do not use lifts. Lie under something sturdy, like a table or desk.

☆ BEWARE the eye of the storm. This is the very centre of the hurricane, which can be very calm. You might think the hurricane is over, but it isn't and more VERY high winds could follow.

Quicksand can suck you under in ten seconds flat

You've seen it at the movies — anyone silly enough to cross quicksand is immediately sucked into its sandy depths. Yikes.

'Can someone pass me my hat?'

And the truth is...

Quicksand is simply a mixture of sand and clay that's so waterlogged it is no longer firm enough to support a person's weight. People who have experienced quicksand describe it as like standing on a jelly. If you move, the surrounding area actually wobbles. But quicksand will *not* suck you right under. If you do sink into quicksand, struggling to get out just means that you dig yourself in deeper. What you should actually do is move your legs very gently to create a gap between them. Water can then flow downwards into the gap and loosen the sand beneath your feet, so you can pull them free. It takes time to get out in this way, but it can be done. And it means that no one will need to lie down on the quicksand and pull you out with a great big, sticky SLURP like they do at the movies.

Verdict: ___ **BUSTED** ___

BEWARE

of quicksand at the seaside.

If you get your feet stuck and the tide comes in, there is a very real danger of drowning.

DON'T eat the liver of a husky dog...

...or a polar bear, or a walrus or a seal because you think it might be full of nutrients. It's actually full of vitamin A, which can kill you, like it did Swiss explorer Xavier Mertz on an Antarctic expedition in 1913.

After eating a husky dog, including its liver, to survive, Mertz became horribly ill. His skin began to peel off, he became weak and delirious. And then he died, probably from hypervitaminosis A, which means too much vitamin A.

The Mertz Glacier in Antarctica is named after him.

DO eat like a pig if you're an Arctic explorer.

It takes a LOT of calories to survive in sub-zero temperatures. Arctic (and Antarctic) explorers gobble about 3,700 calories of food a day to replace lost energy and to keep out the cold, which is nearly twice as much as an adult usually needs to keep them going. That means huge quantities of biscuits and chocolate. BRRRilliant.

DO THIS!

PEMMICAN

Why not make your own delicious and nutritious Arctic (or Antarctic) snack? Pemmican is a traditional high-energy food eaten by all the best explorers.

You will need:

Beef, bison, deer or elk, animal fat, cranberries

What to do:

1. Dry the meat, then pound it into a powder.

2. Heat the fat and mix it with the meat powder.

3. Add a handful of dried cranberries.

4. Pour the meaty, fatty, fruity mixture into a container and wait until it cools and goes hard.

5. Cut the pemmican into pieces.

6. Eat it outside on a winter's day to recreate the magic of the North (or South) Pole.

Yummy! (If you like that sort of thing.)

All snakes are killers

We all know that snakes are right up there with sharks when it comes to having a bad reputation! But did you know that snakes are actually a whole lot more dangerous? The World Health Organization (WHO) estimates that every year, snakes bite at least 421,000 people, which is more than the population of the island of Malta! But the figure could be much higher than this...

★ And the truth is...

The WHO also estimates that at least 20,000 people die from snakebites every year. This means that fewer than 5% of those who suffer snakebites will die, which are pretty good odds ... unless you are bitten by the legendary black mamba, that is. Without anti-venom, given quickly, the black mamba's bite means certain death.

Verdict: **BUSTED** (unless it's a black mamba!)

You can survive without food for two months

Rubbish. Humans need food to survive, don't they? And after two months without food, you'd surely be able to go to a Hallowe'en party as a skeleton — without dressing up.

⭐ And the truth is...

Experts think that you *can* survive for up to two months without food, but — and it's a massive, sodden, dripping-wet 'but' — you DO need water. After just five days without water, you will probably die. Even worse, if you're somewhere very hot, like inside a car on a sweltering summer day, or you're doing strenuous exercise like running a marathon or climbing Everest and not drinking water, your life expectancy plummets to just hours...

Bet you feel thirsty now, right?

Verdict:  **TRUTH**

⭐ Don't put yourself in danger. Stay on the beaten track and totally avoid areas where avalanche warnings have been issued.

⭐ If you are caught in an avalanche, try to grab hold of a tree to stop yourself being dragged along with the speeding snow.

⭐ Cup a hand around your face before the snow stops moving and sets rock hard. Then you'll have a little room to breathe.

⭐ Don't waste your air. Wait until you can hear rescuers on top of you and THEN shout for help.

⭐ If they're dug out within 15 minutes, more than 90% of avalanche victims will survive. If you carry or wear an avalanche-rescue-system receiver, which uses radar technology, it will be much easier for rescue teams to find you.

> In an avalanche, you can save your life by spitting

Ew. Gross. How rude. That's not the sort of behaviour we want to be encouraging in plucky survivors.

★ And the truth is...

If you are buried in an avalanche and you don't know whether you're upside down or the right way up ... SPIT. It will trickle downwards, so you can work out which way is up and so which way to start digging. Don't worry about being polite. And don't worry that it makes you look gross. Do it. If you are buried in an avalanche...

Verdict: _____ TRUTH _____

I'm a survivor!

Joe Simpson and Simon Yates were on their way back down the 6,344-metre-high Siula Grande in the Peruvian Andes, when Joe slipped and fell, breaking his leg. With darkness and bad weather approaching, the pair needed to get down the mountain, fast. Simon lowered Joe on a rope, but visibility was so bad that he didn't realise he was lowering his partner over a cliff and the rope was too short to lower Joe to the bottom.

Simon couldn't pull Joe back up the cliff. Joe couldn't climb up. They were stuck. Even worse, Simon was starting to lose his grip on the mountain. If he didn't do something quickly, they'd both die.

So Simon cut the rope.

Joe plunged into an icy crevasse.

He was DOOMED

Except, he wasn't.

Unbelievably, Joe survived. He'd fallen onto a tiny ledge and used his bit of rope to abseil down the rest of the crevasse. Then he dragged himself and his broken leg back to base camp. And then he wrote down the whole amazing story in *Touching the Void*, which became a bestseller.

The weird thing is that if Simon hadn't cut the rope, both men would probably have plummeted to their deaths. By cutting it, he saved them both.

You can eat human flesh to survive

Mmm. Twice-roasted belly of human with a cream sauce, roast potatoes and green beans. How utterly delicious!

★ And the truth is...

Unless cannibalism becomes really popular, dishes like this won't be appearing on a menu any time soon. But in extreme situations, humans *have* been known to eat each other.

Take the Andes flight disaster, for example. On 13 October, 1972, a rugby team and their friends and family were flying from Montevideo in Uruguay to Santiago in Chile when their aeroplane crashed. There were 45 people on board, but 12 died in the crash and the survivors existed in Arctic conditions until their rescue over two months later. Only 16 people made it, and all admitted that they'd had to eat the victims to survive.

Verdict: **TRUTH**

> # Mosquitoes are more deadly than crocodiles

There's no comparison, surely. Mosquitoes are tiny, annoying creatures whose job is to bite you on holiday and turn you into an itching wreck! Crocodiles are enormous, scary beasts with big, snapping jaws that bite you on safari and turn you into lunch. Which one would YOU prefer to meet?

★ And the truth is...

Crocodiles might kill hundreds of people every year, but mosquitoes are *way* deadlier. It's not a mosquito's blood-sucking bite you need to worry about. Yes, it can leave a nasty swelling and be horribly itchy for a few days. But it's actually diseases such as malaria and dengue fever, which infected mosquitoes carry from one victim to another, that cause the most harm to humans. Experts say that at least 1 million people die from malaria each year — some put the estimate at 2.7 million.

Verdict:  TRUTH

27

...A HOUSE FIRE

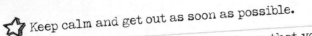

⭐ Keep calm and get out as soon as possible.

⭐ Close any open doors. Only open doors that you need to go through. This will stop the fire spreading quickly.

⭐ If there is a lot of smoke, crawl to avoid breathing it in.

⭐ On your way out, touch each door with the back of your hand before opening it. If the door feels hot, go a different way.

⭐ If you can't get out safely, put bedding or towels along the bottom of the door to seal the gap. This prevents smoke and fumes from getting into the room. Open the window and stay near it so that you can breathe fresh air. Shout, 'FIRE!' to alert other people.

⭐ Make sure that young children know they should try to find a way out of a building if they can, instead of hiding from a fire.

⭐ If there is a lift, do NOT use it. Use the stairs.

⭐ Arrange for everyone to go at a special meeting place outside. Then stay there. Do not go back inside the building.

⭐ Dial 999.

Approved by the London Fire Brigade

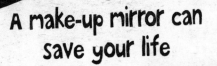

A make-up mirror can save your life

Wow. She's dazzling!

Whaaat? How can something you use to check your favourite sky-blue eyeshadow be used as a life-saving device? Well, aside from reflecting your beeeeautiful face, mirrors are also pretty good at reflecting light. And the sun is the biggest and best light you're ever going to find. So the next time you're stranded on a desert island and you want to attract the attention of the rescue plane or — if you're *really* lucky — helicopter overhead, then wiggle your mirror about so that it catches the sunlight and reflects it right back at your rescuers. Ting!

Yooo-hoo!

Verdict: **TRUTH**

PS If you don't have a mirror handy, just find something shiny to use instead, like a metal flask, a fizzy-drink can, a belt buckle, a shiny badge or sunglasses with mirror lenses.

You need to boil stagnant water for ten minutes for it to be drinkable

Picture the scene... You've just escaped from a burning plane wreck and hiked across muddy swamps and a ravine or two and scaled a couple of cliffs and you're very, very thirsty. (You're probably James Bond too, if you can do all that.) Then you find a lovely pond filled with water. Hurray! The water's a bit green and murky, but you are tempted to drink it anyway.

What do you do?

⭐ And the truth is...

You can never tell what might be lurking in water; disease-causing organisms, pathogens and things that not even scientists can spell. So it's not a good idea to drink stagnant water. But if you have the equipment to hand, there is a VERY easy way of making any water safe to drink. Boil it. Well, technically, 85°C is hot enough, but if you've escaped from a burning plane wreck, you might not have a thermometer handy. And the fact is you don't have to boil the water for ten minutes. Bring it to a rolling boil, let it cool a bit and then get drinking.

Verdict:

BUSTED

I'm a survivor!

Robinson Crusoe by Daniel Defoe is the classic story of the most famous castaway ever. Shipwrecked and stranded on a desert island, Crusoe is stuck there for 28 years before he finds a way home. It sounds so unbelievable that you might think it's totally made-up, right? Wrong. Robinson Crusoe was based on the true story of Alexander Selkirk. The son of a Scottish shoemaker, Selkirk was marooned on an island near Chile in 1704 for four l-o-n-g years. He survived by eating goat, wild turnip and cabbage. Mmm.

If you're stranded on a desert island, spell out HELP in stones

Well, why not? You've probably got a lot of time on your hands. And if you can find enough stones or logs or other objects that can be seen from a rescue plane high above, then pick a big open area, like the beach, and go for it. But is it the best way of being spotted…?

⭐ And the truth is...

It wouldn't do any harm. But a better idea would be to light a fire. And an even better idea would be to light three fires in the shape of a triangle. This is an international distress signal, so anyone who spots it will know at once that you need help. Also, fires will be visible much further away than a load of stones.

Verdict: but light fires too

33

5 ways to... FIND NORTH

OK, you might not always want to travel north, but if you
know where it is, you can work out where east, west and
south are, too. And then you can go ANYWHERE.

1 On a sunny day, poke a stick in the ground. Mark where
the shadow falls. Wait ten minutes while the shadow
moves from east to west. Mark the new position. Draw a
line between the two marks. Stand on the line, with the
first mark (which is west) on your left and the second
mark (east) on your right. Got all that? Good. Then north
is straight ahead. But... if you don't have a stick, go to
number 2.

2 Find an analogue watch — a digital watch will
be no use at all. Point the hour hand towards the
sun. Now work out a place halfway between the
12 and the hour hand. This is the north-south line.
But... if it's cloudy, go to number 3.

3 Find a tree with an anthill near it. Anthills are
usually on the south side of the tree. So north
will be on the other side. But... if you can't find an
anthill, go to number 4.

4 Wait for a starry night. Find the North Star or the Southern Cross constellation, depending on which part of the world you're in. Then find an astronomer to help you with the rest, because this method is really very tricky. Or go to number 5.

5 Use a compass, of course. That's why they were invented.

'Erm, so which way is North then Dave?'

Treat a burn with butter

Accidents happen. And they're not always as extreme as the falling-down-a-crevasse-into-a-crocodile's-open-jaws sort of accident. Sometimes, they're boring old campfire incidents where someone burns themselves on a sausage that is as hot as the core of the sun. But like extreme accidents, burns can hurt too. So how do you treat them? Do you smear butter on a burn, like older and supposedly wiser people say…?

★ And the truth is…

DON'T DO IT. It's an old wives' tale. Greasy stuff like butter will simply keep a burn warm. And that's the very last thing you want to do. What you should do is take the heat away from a burn by holding it under running cool or lukewarm water for at least ten minutes.

Verdict: _____ Totally

36

> # In an extreme survival situation, sawing off your arm could save your life.*

No, no, no, no, no. And again, **no.**

★ And the truth is...

Yes. But it is only true in **VERY** extreme cases, such as the terrible situation in which Aron Ralston found himself in 2003. While hiking in Utah, USA, Ralston disturbed a boulder, which then fell onto him, trapping his right hand. After spending three days trying to move the boulder, he realised that he was never going to shift it and would have to saw his arm off instead. Or die.

It wasn't easy. (If you are at all squeamish, skip to page 40!) As well as cutting through skin and sinew with a blunt knife, he had to snap his own bones too. OUCH. But he did it. And then he climbed down a 20-metre cliff, where he was rescued by helicopter. The events were made into an award-winning film called *127 hours* (2010), which is how long Ralston's ordeal lasted.

Verdict: TRUTH

*But DON'T try this at home.

Turn over for more gory amputations!

Five more people who saved their own lives by amputating a limb...

1 When Sampson Parker's right hand became trapped in the rollers of a corn-picker and he was slowly being dragged into the machine, the American farmer knew it was a matter of life or death. If he didn't act quickly, the burning machine would eat him alive. So he cut off his arm and survived!

2 In 1993, Donald Wyman was felling a huge oak tree when it fell onto him, breaking his leg and trapping it too. Figuring that he might bleed to death before he was discovered, he cut off his own leg below the knee, dragged himself to his bulldozer, drove the bulldozer to his truck, drove that to his friend's house and then asked for help. Wow.

3 Californian Al Hill did the same in 2007 when a tree that he was felling fell on him. Like Donald Wyman, he cut off his own leg.

4 In 2003, an Australian coal miner's arm became trapped under a digger, underground. So he cut it off.

5 When Bill Jeracki was fishing in Colorado, a boulder pinned his left leg. Knowing that snow was forecast, he calmly cut off his leg at the knee joint. He now runs a company that makes artificial limbs.

> **It was all thanks to emergency chocolate supplies that the Apollo 13 astronauts survived their ordeal**

When the Apollo 13 space mission developed a critical fault — an oxygen tank exploded, sending temperatures plummeting and hitting the power supply on board the spacecraft — the three astronauts on board had to keep up their spirits and their energy. So they ate a lot of chocolate.

Mmm. It would be lovely to think so, wouldn't it?

★ And the truth is...

Of course not. The Apollo astronauts relied on essentials like power, water and oxygen to get them out of trouble. Not chocolate*. So the next time you're heading into space or into the rainforest or to a campsite, do make sure you take the right sort of emergency supplies. You'll be glad you did.

* There was no chocolate on spaceships in the 1970s anyway. It was all dull, freeze-dried stuff in pouches.

Verdict: —  —

I'm a survivor!

When a rock fall caused a tunnel to collapse, trapping 33 Chilean miners underground, everyone feared the worst. And for 17 days, no one knew if they were dead or alive. Then rescuers found a note tied to a drill they'd plunged into the mine and knew that the miners were alive. Hurray! It took another agonising 52 days to drill a rescue shaft. Boo! But on 13 October 2010, 69 days after they were buried alive, the 33 miners were all brought to the surface in a 24-hour rescue that was watched live on television all around the world. They became known as 'Los 33'.

DON'T DO THAT...

DON'T stare at a bear...

It's a sign of aggression and the bear will think you want a fight. And you really don't want to get into a fight with a bear. Instead, look down and back slowly away to show the bear that you're not a threat. It's also a good idea to speak in a very calm, very dull voice, not to bore the bear to sleep, but to show that you're a human and someone really not worth fighting. Do try to avoid yelling, 'ARRRRRRGGGGGHHHHH!' That's really not going to help at all.

DO THIS!

DO <u>stare</u> at an alligator

It's true. The best way of escaping an alligator is to stare into its eyes. Just ask the Seminole Indians of Florida, USA, who are experts at this type of thing.

This is what you do:

> Stare at the alligator until it falls into a trance.

> Hold its jaw shut, then roll the deadly creature onto its back and stroke its tummy until it's really, really dopey.

> RUN AWAY.

If you see water in a desert, ALWAYS head towards it

Oh, come on. If you saw a lovely big pool of gently rippling water in the middle of a desert and you were GASPING for a drink, of course you would head towards it, right?

And the truth is...

Don't do it. It's probably a mirage — an optical illusion in which warm air bends light rays to show a wibbly image of the sky that looks just like a pool of water. You're better off heading for an oasis. This is a bunch of palm trees, usually growing around a spring or another water source. And real water is so much more thirst-quenching than the imaginary sort.

Verdict: _BUSTED_

> ## Wearing wet underpants on your head could save your life

Or wear a hat. Whichever's easiest.

★ And the truth is...

Exposure to the sun is one of the two biggest dangers in a desert. (The other is dehydration.) To avoid it, the best thing to do is to stay out of the sun completely. But if you're riding a camel on one of those big wavy sand dunes, that could be tricky. So covering your head is the next best thing. If you haven't got a hat, wrap something around your head instead, to keep the sun off it. Or your pants. Wet underpants would be even cooler. You might look like an idiot but it could save your life!

Verdict: TRUTH

(But take plenty of water, too.)

I'm a survivor!

In October 2010, three teenage boys set sail in a tiny boat in the South Pacific Ocean. They were heading for a nearby island, but somehow lost their way. When they failed to arrive at their destination, everyone thought they'd drowned. In fact, their families were so convinced of this that they held a memorial service for the boys. But they were very much alive. They'd survived by drinking rainwater and eating coconuts, raw fish and a seabird that was foolish enough to land on their boat. After fifty days at sea, the three teenagers were rescued by a fishing trawler. They were very thin, very thirsty, very sunburnt and an astonishing 1,300 kilometres off course.

A coconut tree is the most useful thing on a desert island

Really? Coconut trees look lovely and coconut milk *is* a bit special — *mmmm!* — and a coconut shy at the fair would be pretty rubbish without coconuts, but are they actually useful?

★ And the truth is...

The coconut tree is also known as the tree of life. It has everything a shipwrecked castaway might need for survival. There are materials for building and for clothes. There's firewood. And coconuts themselves are filled with food (coconut flesh) and drink (delicious coconut milk). Find a coconut tree and you're pretty much sorted.

(And then you might as well make clippity-clopping noises with the leftover coconut shells. Because, let's face it, you're probably going to be there for a while. You might need a bit of entertainment to keep your spirits up.)

Verdict: Actually... **BUSTED**

A coconut tree is the *second* most useful thing on a desert island. The most useful thing is a knife. If you haven't got one of those, how are you going to tap open a coconut?

5 ways to... BUILD A RAFT

Whether you're escaping a sinking cruise liner, trying to cross a raging torrent or just need to get from one side of a river to another, a raft will certainly come in handy. So find out how to make one here...

1 Log rafts have been popular for centuries. Why? Because wood floats. (Some wood, that is. Do not make a raft out of mahogany, which is very dense and heavy.)
TOP RAFT TIP: if you've survived a shipwreck, look out for a lump of wood and hang on tight!

2 Wooden rafts are good, but if you want to carry more people or stuff, or would just like to make your raft more stable in rough seas, you will need to add a lighter, more buoyant material ... like polystyrene. This floats really well, for a while. But then it becomes waterlogged and sinks.
TOP RAFT TIP: do not use for long journeys, such as crossing the Atlantic.

3 Or use empty plastic bottles to make your raft more buoyant.
TOP RAFT TIP: make sure that you screw the lids on tightly. Or you will sink.

4 Do you have a stack of spare pig bladders? Excellent. Blow them up and use them to float your raft.
TOP RAFT TIP: when you reach land, celebrate your arrival with a game of football, using one of the pig's bladders. They're THAT useful.

5 Before you get anywhere near water, buy a canoe, of course. That's why they were invented.

A school of piranhas can strip a cow to the bone in under a minute

Wow. That's a pretty amazing claim. But are piranhas really that savage? And if you tried to swim across a river full of piranha fish, would you be history?

50

⭐ And the truth is...

Piranhas have a reputation for being the thugs of the fish world. They don't just eat prey, they RIP IT TO SHREDS with their tiny, triangular, razor-sharp teeth.

Can piranhas strip a cow to the bone? Yes. US president Theodore Roosevelt saw it happen on a visit to Brazil, but the piranha feeding frenzy was a set-up. Local people dumped a heap of very hungry piranhas into the Amazon river ... followed by a cow. It's no wonder the fish devoured the poor creature.

In true life, piranhas usually swim alone and although they do have a big appetite, they have a balanced diet of fish, fruit and seeds. They rarely attack cows or people.

And what about swimming across that piranha-infested river? Actually, you can. But if you're going to do it, do it at night. Piranhas hunt in the daytime and sleep at night. And if awakened, they'll usually swim away rather than devour you with their razor-sharp teeth. Swim by moonlight and all you have to do is avoid all the other dangerous things in the water.

Or go by boat.

Verdict: **BUSTED**

☆ Keep alert for tsunami warnings on TV and radio.

☆ Watch the sea. If the water suddenly pulls back and you can see a lot of beach, this could mean that a tsunami is on the way.

☆ Watch pets and other animals. If they start to act strangely, this may also be a sign that a tsunami is about to happen.

☆ Head inland. The further away from the sea you are, the longer it will take the tsunami to reach you and the safer you will be.

☆ If you can't move inland, get as high as you can, even if it means climbing onto a roof.

☆ If there are no buildings nearby, as a last resort, climb a sturdy tree.

☆ If you are caught in a tsunami, grab hold of anything that floats and don't let go.

> ## Being stranded on a desert island is like the best holiday ever

'What do you mean it's coconut for dinner AGAIN?'

Just imagine...
beautiful sandy
beaches, palm trees
and endless sunshine...
Fancy being able to
go swimming all day,
every day.
Brilliant!

★ And the truth is...

Castaways aren't usually stranded on a desert island for a fortnight. Just ask Alexander Selkirk on page 32. And a proper desert island doesn't have a restaurant, a disco, a pool complex and a local band playing live every Friday. It's more like solitary confinement in a prison, but without the regular meals. You have to find *those* for yourself. Good luck!

Verdict:  BUSTED

...AN EARTHQUAKE

IF YOU ARE INDOORS...

⭐ Stay there.

⭐ Find somewhere safe to shelter. Good places are under a strong desk or table, in a doorway or near an inside wall.

⭐ Do not shelter near windows, heavy furniture, large mirrors or other objects that might fall onto you.

IF YOU ARE OUTDOORS...

⭐ Move to an open area, where falling objects won't crush you.

⭐ Stay away from buildings, telephone and electricity lines, trees and large signs.

⭐ Do not shelter on or under bridges, during an earthquake. There is a possibility that they will collapse.

All scorpions are DEADLY

Scorpions are the bad guys of the arthropod world. They have eight legs, evil-looking claws and a nasty sting in their curved tail. In films, all scorpions are deadly. Even film star spies are scared of them. But are they really so bad?

★ And the truth is...

No, they aren't. Scorpions do not usually go looking for a fight. They wait for prey to come to them. And they are most active at night, so unless you are an insomniac, you're unlikely to meet one. As for their poisonous tails, of the 1,750 species of scorpion, only 25 are armed with venom that is deadly to humans. And of all people stung by scorpions every year, fewer than 0.5% actually die. So the risk of being killed by a scorpion is very, very small.

Verdict: — BUSTED —

A pair of tights can be used to fix your car in the desert

Tights, stockings, pop socks, pantyhose or whatever you call them are supposed to come in really handy if your car breaks down in the middle of nowhere. But do they really work?

And the truth is...

The pulleys — small wheels — that used to pull a fan belt around an engine to power the fan and other vital engine components once had a v-shaped groove around the outside rim. The thin fan belt fitted into this groove perfectly. So, if the fan belt snapped, it just *might* have been possible to use a pair of tights in its place. But a car repaired in this way would only have been able to travel a VERY short distance, perhaps to the nearest garage. A pair of tights would not be strong or durable enough to get a car out of a desert.

With a modern car, you're totally stuffed. The serpentine belt — so called because it snakes around the engine — is virtually impossible to reach because of the car's design. And the pulleys are the wrong shape anyway.

So if you break down in the desert, you're better off just ringing for a breakdown truck on your mobile.

Or hitching a ride on a camel.

Verdict:

unless you're
driving a vintage
car 500 metres
down the road

Bonus tights tip: *If you ladder your tights attempting to fix an old car, you can stop the hole getting any bigger by daubing on clear nail varnish. That's your car and your tights fixed. And you're welcome.*

A foil blanket might save your life

Yeah, right.
Foil is for Christmas
turkeys, *not* people.

BAN
CHRISTMAS!

★ **And the
truth is...**
Believe it or not, foil
blankets — or 'space
blankets' as the
experts like to call
them — come in really
handy in emergency
situations. They are
not made of kitchen foil because that would rip really easily.
Space blankets are actually thin sheets of plastic covered with
a shiny coating that reflects body heat to regulate a person's
temperature. This might help an athlete who's run a marathon
— whose body temperature can plummet after a race — and
also keep people warm and dry in disaster situations.

Verdict: _____ TRUTH

I'm a survivor!

The very worst, most catastrophically terrible and totally, truly awful thing that can happen to a bungee jumper is when their cord SNAPS. Or is it? Australian backpacker Erin Langworthy might disagree. When she bungee-jumped from the Victoria Falls Bridge in Zambia, the cord snapped, which was bad. But then Erin plunged into the crocodile-infested waters of the Zambezi river, which was worse. Worse still, her feet were tied together with the remains of the bungee rope, which made it really difficult to swim – then the rope got caught on underwater rocks, making it even trickier. Amazingly, Erin swam to safety.

DON'T take ponies on an expedition to the South Pole.

It sounds a bit bizarre, doesn't it? Who would take lovely, prancing ponies to one of the most inhospitable places on earth and then make them carry all the gear? Robert Falcon Scott of the Antarctic, that's who.

A century ago, when the famous British explorer set off to conquer the South Pole, he decided to take 20 Siberian ponies with him. The idea was that the ponies would carry food and equipment for the first half of the journey. Then, when the journey got colder and tougher, the explorers would take over and carry everything. Sadly, the ponies that didn't die of exhaustion were eaten by dogs and killer whales. And even though Scott's expedition did reach the South Pole on 17 January 1912, all five of the brave explorers died on the way back.

DO THIS!

DO take dogs on an expedition to the South Pole.

At almost exactly the same time that Scott set off for the South Pole, so did Norwegian explorer Roald Amundsen. But instead of taking ponies, Amundsen took 52 sledge dogs on the tough journey. The dogs pulled four sledges across the icy-cold landscape, which was hard work. But Amundsen looked after his animals, making sure that they got enough rest and that they ate well, feasting on seals and penguins on the way. When they reached the final stage of the journey, 27 of the remaining dogs were killed for food.

On 14 December 1911, Roald Amundsen and his party won the race to the South Pole. Afterwards, all of the party returned safely home.

> # Frostbite causes your fingers or toes to turn black and drop off

Frostbite happens when parts of the body are affected by very low temperatures. Extremities — pointy bits such as noses, fingers and toes — are usually the first to suffer because they are the furthest points from a person's heart. But any skin that is exposed to extreme cold can also be frostbitten.

★ And the truth is...

The first stage of frostbite is when a person suffers itching and pain. Then, their skin turns white, red and yellow and becomes numb. Next, it freezes and goes hard. Finally, if frostbite is *still* left untreated, everything freezes — muscles, blood vessels and nerves, EVERYTHING. This is when toes and fingers go purple, then black and there's a danger of gangrene, which is when the body starts to go rotten. The offending finger or toe won't drop off, but it *will* need to be amputated.

Verdict: Mostly **TRUTH**   but only if the frostbite is very bad

62

Climbing Mount Everest can make you sick

Oh, dear. That doesn't sound good. Surely climbing the highest mountain in the world is tough enough already without having to cope with being sick on the way.

Lovely view darling...

...Burp!

⭐ And the truth is...

Altitude sickness is a condition that can happen when someone is very high up. Sufferers may have difficulty breathing (because there is less oxygen the higher you go), headaches, dizziness, exhaustion and nausea. Bleurgh.

The way to avoid altitude sickness is not to climb a mountain too quickly. If you begin to feel ill, stay where you are until you recover. Or go a little lower until the symptoms subside. And if you go slowly, you really will feel on top of the world when you reach the summit.

Verdict: _____

TRUTH

> If you visit the Arctic Circle, you can stay warm in a 5-star hotel

That's absolutely nuts, surely. Why would anyone bother building a hotel in one of the most inhospitable places on earth, never mind offering holidays to *stay* in one?

★ And the truth is...

ICEHOTEL is in Jukkasjärvi, a small village in Lapland, Finland. It's 200 kilometres north of the Arctic Circle. However, its location is not the most amazing thing about this hotel. It's the fact that it's made from ice and snow. ICEHOTEL is only open from December to April, the darkest time of year in the Arctic Circle, when the sun barely rises above the horizon, even during the daytime. And because the hotel melts when the weather warms up in spring, this means that a new hotel is built every single year. How cool is that? Get it? Cool? COOL?! Oh never mind.

Verdict: TRUTH

Five more mad, scary and downright BIZARRE places to enjoy a holiday!

1. The Water Discus Hotel has been designed to look like a spaceship, no less! When it's built in Dubai, half of the hotel will be above the sea and half below the waves, where the underwater guests will enjoy a beautiful fishy view.

2. The Jumbo Stay Hotel in Stockholm, Sweden is nothing to do with elephants. It's a vintage 747 jumbo jet that has been converted into a hotel.

3. The Palacio de Sal is a hotel in Bolivia, South America made entirely of salt.

4. The Sala Silvermine in Sweden is a B&B with a difference. Its one suite is 155 metres underground.

5. The Baumhaus Hotel in Neißeaue, Germany is a collection of treehouses. It is not recommended if you are afraid of heights. Or trees.

> # If your parachute doesn't deploy, you will plummet to your death

It's basic science, isn't it? If your parachute breaks or doesn't even open in the first place, then you're stuffed. Or, rather, squashed. By the time you hit the ground, you'll be going so fast that the impact will kill you.

★ And the truth is...

Not always. If you're lucky, the back-up chute will work and you'll be fine. But even when that's broken, parachutists have survived VERY long falls, like UK cameraman Paul Lewis. In 2009, he was skydiving when both his main parachute *and* his reserve parachute failed. He crashed onto the roof of an aircraft hangar — and survived!

Verdict:  sometimes!

If you fall out of an aeroplane, you will die

Unless you're wearing a parachute, of course. And if that parachute opens properly. (If it doesn't, see page 66.) Then you're pretty much guaranteed to reach the ground in one piece. But what about those poor air passengers who fall from the sky WITHOUT a parachute? They don't stand a chance, right?

 And the truth is...

Falling out of an aeroplane is never a good idea. Usually, it's GAME OVER. Usually ... but not always. A lucky few have left their aircraft in mid-air and lived to tell the tale. Ideally, plummeting people should aim for a snowdrift or a rainforest or the sea. And they should also make sure that they have a **LOT** of luck.

Turn over for some amazing falls!

Verdict:  BUSTED sometimes!

~~I'm a~~ We're survivors!

1 In 1943, American airman Alan Magee survived a 6,700-metre fall into occupied France and through the glass roof of a railway station. He broke bones, suffered head injuries and nearly lost an arm, but lived.

2 When Joe Herman's bomber was hit in 1944, he was blown clear. As the Australian airman fell, he caught hold of something falling beside him. And luckily for Herman it was not something, but someone. The someone was John Vivash, who pulled his ripcord and the two men floated down to earth together. Both survived.

3 Also in 1944, RAF airman Nicholas Alkemade jumped out of a burning aircraft over Germany, without a parachute. He fell nearly 5,500 metres onto a perfect winter's scene of trees and fluffy snow. And all he did was sprain his leg.

4 Air stewardess Vesna Vulovic was on board an aircraft when it exploded over the former Czechoslovakia in 1972. The aeroplane broke into pieces and fell over 10 kilometres to the ground. Vulovic landed safely, still inside a section of the fuselage. She was badly injured, but survived and made a good recovery.

5 In 1942, Russian airman Ivan Chisov bailed out of his bombed aircraft at 7,000 metres, but decided that if he deployed his parachute, he'd draw attention to himself and would be shot down AGAIN. But then he passed out and couldn't pull the ripcord. He landed in a snowy ravine and rolled to the bottom. He survived.

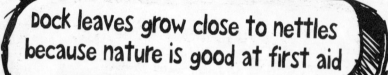

Dock leaves grow close to nettles because nature is good at first aid

If you've ever been stung by stinging nettles, you'll know that they hurt, lots. But did you know that wherever there are nettles you're also likely to find dock leaves? If you rub one of these beauties on your nettle sting, it really will make it feel a little better. But why are dock leaves found near nettles? Is nature really that thoughtful?

Nettle

★ And the truth is...

Dock leaves are a traditional remedy for nettle stings, but the only reason that they are found near each other is because they both thrive in overgrown habitats.

Verdict:  BUSTED

If you've run out of water, just drink your wee

Urgh. No thanks. Why would anyone even *think* of doing that?

⭐ And the truth is...

Actually, in desperate situations, some people have drunk their own urine. But the jury's out on whether it's a good idea or not, and scientists say that it couldn't possibly be done for a long time because there would be a build-up of toxic substances inside the person's body, which would eventually kill them. A better idea is just to make sure you have enough water in the first place.

Verdict: Sometimes **TRUTH** But don't try this at home.

71

5 ways to... MAKE A FIRE

If you want to eat sausages on a camping trip, you'll need a fire. (And you'll need sausages.) Fires can be extremely dangerous, so make sure that you have an adult's help. To start with you need to make a tinder nest. This is the special survival skills' name for a little pile of grass, leaves or bark. It has to be dry. Otherwise, it won't catch fire. Now, light the tinder nest by using one of these handy methods.

1 Rub two sticks together until you have a tiny flame to light your tinder nest. You do have a few hours spare, right?

2

Focus sunlight through a lens – try a pair of glasses or a magnifying glass – and onto your tinder nest. Like magic, it will catch fire.

3 Use a flint-and-steel set, available in all good camping shops. It's almost as good as having a box of matches.

4 Make a bow drill by threading a wooden stick through a bow, then rolling the bow back and forth to spin the tip of the drill onto a fireboard, to create friction and then fire. Got that? Or...

5 ...buy a box of matches, of course. That's why they were invented.

...A METEORITE STRIKE

★ Don't worry. You have a one in 20 trillion chance of being hit by a meteorite. So it's almost certainly never going to happen.

★ Still don't worry. NASA's Near Earth Object Program is watching the sky right now, so scientists know exactly where the really big meteors or asteroids are and they will warn us if any are likely to hit our planet, so we can get out of the way.

★ Really don't worry. Because even if you are one of the unlucky ones who IS struck by a meteorite, like German schoolboy Gerrit Blank in 2009, then you might still be fine. A pea-sized meteorite bounced off Gerrit's hand and he survived.

★ STILL really don't worry. If a meteorite strike does happen, you're not going to know much about it. Just ask the dinosaurs on the Yucatán Peninsula in Mexico.

Black widow spiders like to hide in shoes

It's a spider's dream hiding place, isn't it? Quiet, dark *and* cosy. And if someone dares to put their foot inside a shoe, it's really, really easy to BITE them.

And the truth is...

Black widow spiders are said to like dry, dark, sheltered places. They have been found under stones and logs, in barns and sheds, around toilet seats and dustbin lids and they've also been found in clothes ... and SHOES. The jury's out on whether a black widow's favourite home of all time is the inside of a smelly old shoe. But if you live in North America, where black widows are common, it might be a good to check your shoes before putting them on. Just in case...

Verdict: TRUTH (but they love a nice shed, too)

You can calculate how far away a storm is by counting the gap between lightning and thunder

That's the saying that you've heard a million times, right? But can it really be as simple as all that?

And the truth is...

Yes. Thunder is simply the sound that lightning makes. They happen at exactly the same time, it's just that lightning travels at the speed of light, which is extraordinarily fast (in fact it is 299,792,458 metres per second), while thunder is v-e-r-y s-l-o-w (only 343.2 metres per second, when the air is very dry), so we always see the flash before we hear the thunder.

We see the lightning before we hear the thunder because light travels faster than sound. The light from the lightning travels to our eyes much quicker than the sound from the lightning so we hear it later than we see it. The nearer a storm is, the less time the thunder takes.

To work out how far away a storm is, all you have to do is count the seconds in between a flash of lightning and the roll of thunder that follows. To get your answer in kilometres per hour, divide the answer by 3. And if you'd prefer your answer in miles per hour, divide your answer by 5.

So, if there are 15 seconds between the lightning and thunder, the storm is 5 kilometres or 3 miles away. Ta-daaaa.

Verdict:

Survival skills fact: Lightning kills or injures more people per year than hurricanes or tornadoes!

...A LIGHTNING STRIKE

☆ If you are outside during a storm, look for shelter. Cars and buildings are good places. Trees are very, very bad.

☆ If you can't find anywhere to shelter, make yourself as small as possible. Crouch down with your feet close together and bend your head forward.

☆ Don't touch your head on the ground. If you're struck by lightning, electricity will travel through your head. And that's never going to end well.

☆ Don't believe the saying that lightning never strikes in the same place twice. It can ... and does.

I'm a Survivor!

Pasquale Buzzelli is one of the luckiest men alive. On 11 September 2001, he survived the collapse of the twin towers of the World Trade Center in New York City. Pasquale was on the 64th floor of the North Tower when it was hit by an aeroplane. He escaped down one of the stairways, but had only reached the 22nd floor when the building began to shake and then collapsed around him. Amazingly, Pasquale surfed through the falling debris and was found sitting atop a pile of rubble when the dust settled. His only injury was a broken leg.

DON'T DO THAT...

DON'T keep lipstick in your tent...

...when you are camping in a wood full of bears. And don't keep any tins of food, drinks, soaps, toiletries, rubbish or dirty dishes in there either. Bears will think it all smells simply irresistible and might break in and try to find it so they can gobble it up. And then they might find you. And gobble you up, too.

PS The author actually did this in Yosemite, USA, but luckily the bears didn't fancy that particular shade of lipgloss and so on that occasion she wasn't eaten and lived to write this book. Phew.

DO THIS!

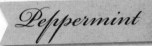

DO plaster yourself with peppermint...

...if there are mosquitoes about. There are certain scents that the pesky insects REALLY don't like. So if you'd like to avoid nasty, itchy mosquito bites, try slathering yourself in any or all of the smells on the right. (The downside? Humans might avoid you, too.)

Lordy!

Peppermint

Citronella

Rosemary

Sage

Lavender

Cinnamon

Garlic

5 ways to... MAKE A WATERPROOF SHELTER

Just imagine. You've been trekking through a rainforest and it's getting dark. Even worse, it's about to rain. (Well, it is a rainforest.) You desperately need a waterproof shelter ... and fast.

1 Make a bivouac by constructing a frame of branches and then covering them with leaves and ferns to keep the rain out.

2 A thatched hut will keep you super dry. First make a domed shelter from bendy branches and then cover them with bundles of grass. But be warned. These take quite a while to make, so you might get soaking wet before you manage to finish it.

3 If you have a tarpaulin handy — call it a tarp, if you want to sound really cool — hang this over a frame of branches. It will make your shelter *really* waterproof.

4 If you don't have a tarpaulin, try a bin bag.

5 Go to the camping shop before you set off on your adventure and buy a tent, of course. That's why they were invented.

I'm a survivor!

Two Norwegian kayakers called Sebastian Plur Nilssen and Ludvig Fjeld wanted to become the first kayakers to paddle around Svalbard in the Arctic. What they didn't want was to be attacked by polar bears. But that's exactly what happened in July 2010, when they were sleeping. The clever polar bears made it past the trip wires that the kayakers had set. One smashed into the tent, clamped its jaws around Sebastian's head, then dragged the unlucky kayaker outside and started to shake him. Ludvig leapt to the rescue and fired a single shot, toppling the bear instantly. Amazingly, Sebastian survived.

If a hippo swallows your head, you're history

Yikes. That's got to hurt, right?

Hippos are HUGE. The very biggest hippos can measure over 4 metres long and weigh up to 3.6 tonnes, which is over five times as much as a Formula One car (including the driver). Their massive jaws are hinged in a way that means they can open them very wide — nearly as much as 180°. And this, of course, is a very useful trick if you want to fit a human head inside. But that's not the scariest bit. A hippo's canine teeth, which can grow up to 50 centimetres long, sharpen themselves as they grind together!

So, when a hippo swallowed Paul Templer's head on the Zambezi river, he must have thought he *was* history.

Wow, it's got dark all of a sudden!

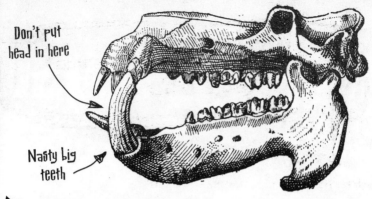

Don't put head in here

Nasty big teeth

★ And the truth is...

It's not a good idea to put your head anywhere near a hippo's jaws, but it doesn't *always* mean certain death. When Paul Templer jumped into the river to save his friend, the hippo swallowed his head. Somehow, Templer managed to pull himself out of the animal's jaws, but the hippo went back to attack him. Templer lost his arm, but he didn't lose his head.

Verdict: **BUSTED** sometimes

⭐ Take Wellington boots. If it rains the ground will instantly change from beautiful, springy grass into gloopy, icky, sticky mud. And it will stay that way until you go home.

⭐ Take waterproofs. See previous point.

⭐ Take a spare toilet roll, in case the festival toilets run out. And you REALLY don't want to be stuck in a festival toilet without toilet paper.

FESTIVAL.

⭐ Take sun cream. This is important. Most festivals are held during summer, so you don't want to be caught out with a nasty case of sunburn. Ouch.

⭐ Take wet wipes. It will save you getting washed properly. Your parents will never know (unless they read this).

⭐ Take earplugs. You might not like ALL of the bands' music and if you pop in a pair of earplugs, no one will know that you can't hear them.

⭐ Take Wellingtons, which are so totally vital that they're worth mentioning twice. And let's face it, it WILL rain.

You can track down water with a bent stick

The ancient art of divining, or dowsing, is supposed to be a way of finding sources of water (and also oil, metal and other substances) that are hidden underground. The water diviner walks around slowly, holding a V-shaped stick and concentrating very hard. When the stick twitches, this indicates that water is nearby.

★ And the truth is...

The jury's out on whether this method of finding water actually works or not. Some people think it does. Many don't. There's no scientific evidence behind it and studies have shown that you have the same chance of finding water by guessing as by divining. If you're likely to be thirsty on your travels, it might be better to pack a couple of bottles of water instead and save yourself the bother of divining for it.

Verdict: Almost definitely **BUSTED**

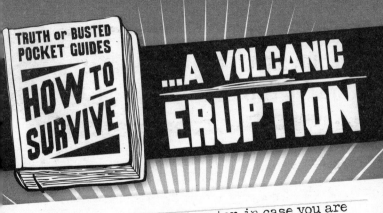

☆ Fill your bath with water, in case you are cut off.

☆ Stay indoors, if at all possible.

☆ If you have to go outside, wear a mask and goggles. This is to keep volcanic ash out of your eyes and lungs.

☆ Don't attempt to outrun lava flow. Instead, climb to higher ground to avoid it.

☆ Don't go sightseeing during a volcanic eruption. It might look amazing, but it is VERY dangerous.

☆ Volcano experts are called volcanologists. Honestly. So, with a name as fabulous as that, if a volcanologist tells you that you're in danger, GET OUT OF THERE.

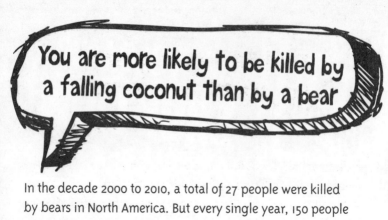

You are more likely to be killed by a falling coconut than by a bear

In the decade 2000 to 2010, a total of 27 people were killed by bears in North America. But every single year, 150 people around the world are killed by falling coconuts

Oops! Do I still get a prize?

★ And the truth is...

It's a fact, people. Coconuts are more dangerous than bears.

Verdict: _____ **TRUTH**

The best way to go over Niagara Falls is in a barrel

Well, travelling by barrel is one way of going over Niagara Falls. And it's a very popular method of waterfall transport for the thrill seeker. But other ways of going over the Niagara Falls have so far included a diving bell, a jet ski and a canoe. And some people have risked their lives in just the clothes they were wearing. So what's the best way to do it?

★ And the truth is...

Those in charge at Niagara Falls would rather that no one went over them at all. Not in a barrel, not in a diving bell, not on a canoe and definitely not without any flotation device at all. The practice is totally illegal and anyone caught — either before or after they go over the edge — is given a hefty fine and sometimes a prison sentence (if they are pulled out alive, of course). This isn't because the authorities are spoilsports. It's because it's a VERY DANGEROUS STUNT.

But, even though it's a VERY DANGEROUS STUNT, going over Niagara Falls is slightly less dangerous if it's done inside a barrel. This is because the barrel gives the person inside some protection from the 110,000 cubic metres of water that fall over the edge every single second and also helps them to survive the 51-metre drop into the pounding surf below.

Turn over for more Niagara 'falls'!

91

Only four people are known to have survived Niagara Falls without a flotation device. (One of these was seven-year-old Roger Woodward, who was accidentally swept over the edge in 1960.) But eleven people made it inside a barrel or a diving bell.

Extra bonus fact!

Did you know that Niagara Falls is not one waterfall, but three? They are the Bridal Veil Falls, the American Falls and — the biggest and most famous of them all — the Horseshoe Falls, which is very popular with daredevils. It's wide and curved like a horseshoe and, most importantly, doesn't have a pile of deadly rocks piled at the bottom of it. Because, let's face it, falling onto those is REALLY going to hurt.

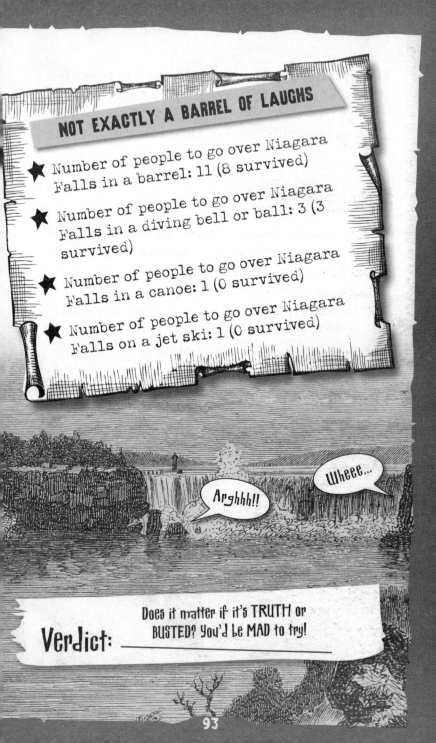

NOT EXACTLY A BARREL OF LAUGHS

★ Number of people to go over Niagara Falls in a barrel: 11 (8 survived)

★ Number of people to go over Niagara Falls in a diving bell or ball: 3 (3 survived)

★ Number of people to go over Niagara Falls in a canoe: 1 (0 survived)

★ Number of people to go over Niagara Falls on a jet ski: 1 (0 survived)

Arghhh!!

Wheee...

Verdict: Does it matter if it's TRUTH or BUSTED? You'd be MAD to try!

Where can I find myths about...

100%
SUCKER-PROOF

GUARANTEED!

Take a look at our other marvellously mythbusting titles...

Tip:
Turn over!

How NOT to be a sucker...

978 0 7502 6959 9

978 0 7502 6958 2

978 0 7502 8155 3

978 0 7502 8158 4

978 0 7502 7081 6

978 0 7502 7915 4

978 0 7502 8157 7

978 0 7502 8159 1

978 0 7502 8131 7

978 0 7502 6957 5

TRUTH or BUSTED

YOU SWALLOW SPIDERS IN YOUR SLEEP!
The fact or fiction behind ANIMALS

MEDIEVAL PEOPLE WASHED THEIR CLOTHES IN WEE!
The fact or fiction behind HISTORY

THE QUEEN LOVED TO SEE SHAKESPEARE'S BOTTOM!
The fact or fiction behind SHAKESPEARE

YOU CAN FILL SWIMMING POOL WITH YOUR SPIT!
The fact or fiction behind HUMAN BODIES

HUMAN BEINGS CAN GO POP IN SPACE!
The fact or fiction behind SCIENCE

YOU CAN GET SUCKED DOWN AN AEROPLANE LOO!
The fact or fiction behind URBAN MYTHS

BUY THEM NOW!

YOU CAN OVERPOWER A CROCODILE WITH AN ELASTIC BAND!
The fact or fiction behind SURVIVAL SKILLS

FOOTBALLERS EARN LESS THAN THEIR UNDERPANTS DO!
The fact or fiction behind FOOTBALL

BLACKBEARD'S HEADLESS BODY SWAM AROUND HIS SHIP!
The fact or fiction behind PIRATES

THE SMELL OF POO CLOSED PARLIAMENT!
The fact or fiction behind LONDON